HEY, YOU!

Poems to Skyscrapers, Mosquitoes, and Other Fun Things

selected by
Paul B. Janeczko

illustrated by
Robert Rayevsky

HarperCollinsPublishers

To the memory of my mother,
Verna Janeczko (1918–2004)
This one's for you, Mom.
Thanks for everything.
—P.B.J.

Library of Congress Cataloging-in-Publication Data is available.
ISBN-10: 0-06-052347-6 — ISBN-13: 978-0-06-052347-3
ISBN-10: 0-06-052348-4 (lib. bdg.) — ISBN-13: 978-0-06-052348-0 (lib. bdg.)

Design by Robert Rayevsky and Martha Rago
1 2 3 4 5 6 7 8 9 10
❖
First Edition

IMAGINATION ON THE LOOSE

Have you ever spoken to your sneakers? Or talked to your mailbox? Sounds wacky, doesn't it? Well, this book is filled with poems that were written *to* things. What kinds of things? How about poems to a fork or an octopus? They're in here. So are poems to mosquitoes and a skyscraper. There's even a poem in this book to the Vietnam Veterans Memorial.

Why would anyone write a poem *to* a thing? Because it's fun! And it can also be a challenge. You need to really observe the thing and discover what you might say to it. Then, of course, you'll need to find the right words to make it come alive.

There is lots of room for imagination when a poet writes to a thing. As you read these poems, let *your* imagination go. You might even want to get out your pencil and paper and write a poem of your own. Give it a try!

CONTENTS

Invocation	George Ella Lyon	5
A Mote of Dust	X. J. Kennedy	6
Sneakers	Joan Bransfield Graham	7
To an Astronaut	Beverly McLoughland	8
Lovely Mosquito	Doug MacLeod	10
Mosquito Mosquito	John Agard	11
Little Blanco River	Naomi Shihab Nye	12
Toad	Norman MacCaig	13
Camel Question	Bobbi Katz	14
Old Farm in Northern Michigan	Gary Gildner	16
To a Maggot in an Apple	Richard Edwards	17
Light	Joan Bransfield Graham	18
Soft-boiled	Russell Hoban	20
Warning to a Fork	Marjorie Maddox	21
Buffalo	Penny Harter	22
Bison	Kristine O'Connell George	23
To a Snowflake	X. J. Kennedy	24
Hat Hair	Joan Bransfield Graham	25
Letter Poem to a Mailbox	Marjorie Maddox	26
Bee, I'm expecting you!	Emily Dickinson	28
Straight Talk	Nikki Grimes	29
Dear shell:	Karla Kuskin	30
Conch Shell	Beverly McLoughland	31
The Octopus	Ogden Nash	32
The Sea Horse	Douglas Florian	33
Skyscraper	Dennis Lee	34
What Are You Doing?	Charles Reznikoff	35
Whispers to the Wall	Rebecca Kai Dotlich	36
Hello, Moon!	Patricia Hubbell	38
Hello, Black Hole	J. Patrick Lewis	40

INVOCATION
George Ella Lyon

O pen, open poem.
O paper, pave the way.
O ink, give me inklings
in your dark tongue
what to say.

O letter, let me draw you
out to shape us,
close to hold.
O word, breathe me onward
into mysteries untold.

O sound, sing me deeper
where the soul is so inclined
that if pen open poem,
poem will open
heart and mind.

A MOTE OF DUST
X. J. Kennedy

Dust-speck in a sunbeam,
I blow a breath. You soar
Revolving like some mighty moon
For spacefolk to explore.

What will you show them? Roads of gold
Where chariots and dragons race?
A princess dressed in spidery silk,
Moonbeams all over her face?

Your people—do they raise tall trees
Or trash heaps? Build or wreck?
Play ball, or play at war to win
The right to rule you, speck?

When, tired of circling in the sun,
You want to spend the night,
Drift down. Take my fingertip
To be your landing site.

SNEAKERS
Joan Bransfield Graham

Sneakers,
glancing from bed,
I see morning light cast
long shadows behind you just like
comets.

Your tails
flaring, you seem
ready to blaze into
the day, either with or without
my feet!

TO AN ASTRONAUT
Beverly McLoughland

When you're in space
So far away
With darkness all around,

And you see the little Earth
Beyond,
Do you miss its windy sound?

Do you feel alone
With endless space
The neighbor at your door?

Do you miss the Earth
So far away?
Do you love it even more?

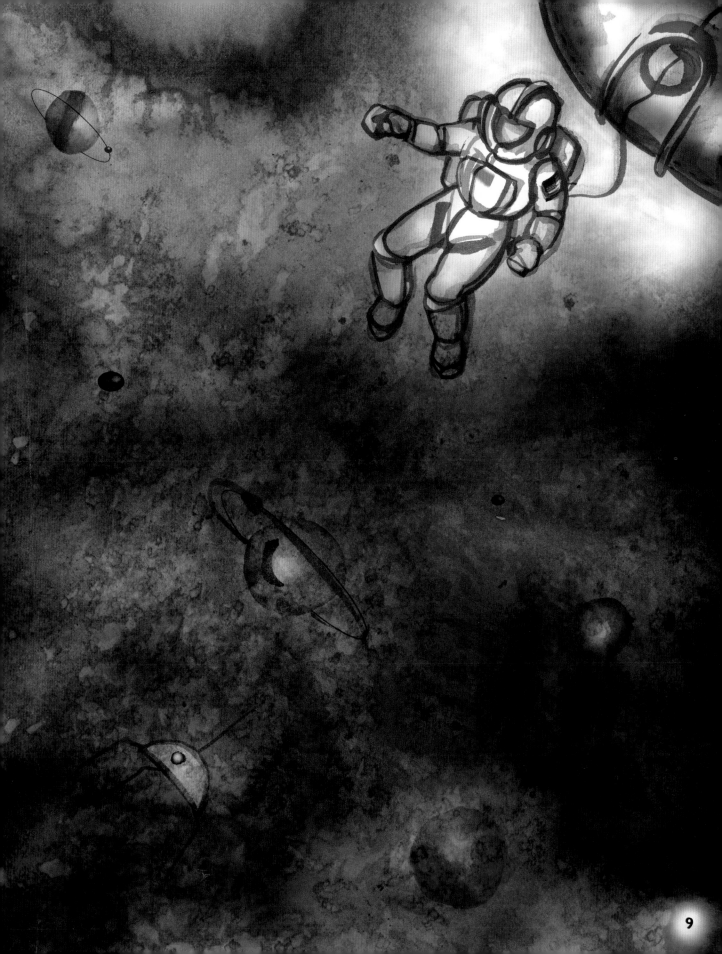

LOVELY MOSQUITO
Doug MacLeod

Lovely mosquito, attacking my arm
As quiet and still as a statue,
Stay right where you are! I'll do you no harm—
I simply desire to pat you.

Just puncture my veins and swallow your fill
For nobody's going to swat you.
Now, lovely mosquito, stay perfectly still—

A SWIPE! and a **SPLAT!** and **I GOT YOU!**

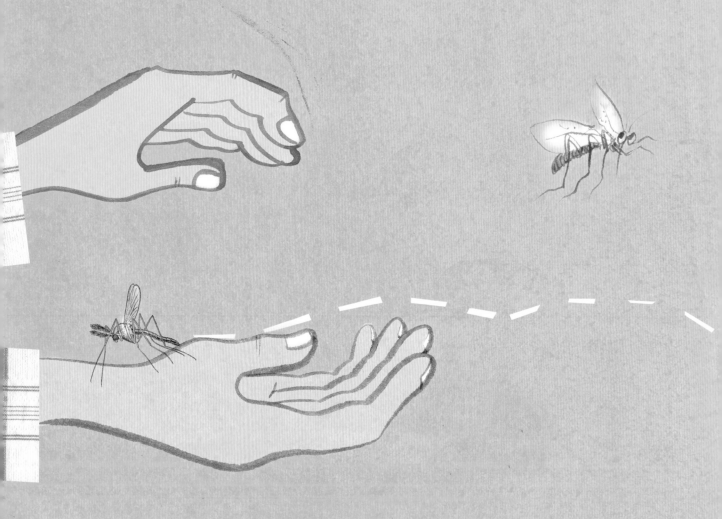

MOSQUITO MOSQUITO

John Agard

Mosquito mosquito, why do you go
     everywhere I go?
Well my child, it's blood I follow.
Mosquito mosquito, biting people, is that all
     you know?
Yes, my child, biting people is all I know.

Well mosquito, don't bite me, bite Uncle Joe.
He always boasting he sweet from head to toe.

LITTLE BLANCO RIVER
Naomi Shihab Nye

You're only a foot deep
under green water
your smooth shale skull
is slick & cool
blue dragonfly
skims you
like a stone
   skipping
    skipping
it never goes under
you square-dance with boulders
make a clean swishing sound
centuries of skirts
lifting & falling in delicate rounds
no one makes a state park out of you
you're not deep enough
little blanco river
don't ever get too big

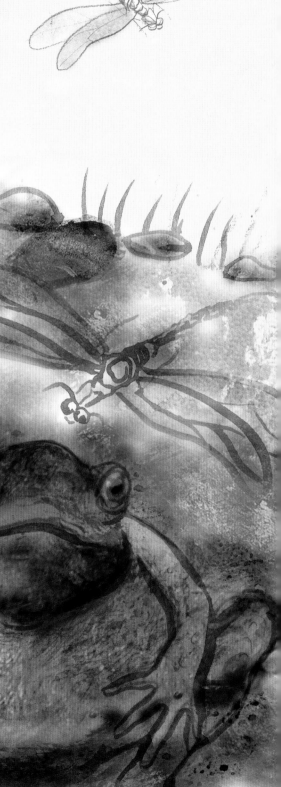

TOAD
Norman MacCaig

Stop looking like a purse. How could a purse
squeeze under the rickety door and sit,
full of satisfaction, in a man's house?

You clamber towards me on your four corners—
one hand, one foot, one hand, one foot.

I love you for being a toad,
for crawling like a Japanese wrestler,
and for not being frightened.

I put you in my purse hand, not shutting it,
and set you down outside directly under
every star.

A jewel in your head? Toad,
you've put one in mine,
a tiny radiance in a dark place.

CAMEL QUESTION
Bobbi Katz

Humpy, bumpy camel,
a sign tells me you bite.
You look so very friendly,
I can't believe you might.
Do you long for palm trees,
sand and an oasis?
I wonder if your hump is stuffed
with dreams of desert places.

OLD FARM IN NORTHERN MICHIGAN
Gary Gildner

Barn, you have leaned too far
trying for those wormy apples.
Now your cows will never come back
and fill their pails with cream.
Now the horse will never come back
with its hot breath and sweaty collar.
Barn, you have leaned too far—
even the cat thinks you are crazy
and stays close to the car.

TO A MAGGOT IN AN APPLE
Richard Edwards

You lie there like a baby,
Frail and soft and curled,
I'm sorry that I broke in
To your safe white world.
I really didn't mean to,
Just blame my appetite
For laying bare your cradle
And letting in the light.
One question then I'll leave you
To slumber in the bin—
I'm feeling rather queasy,
Er . . . did you have a twin?

LIGHT
Joan Bransfield Graham

Light,
 light,
  stretch
   my sight,
    bend back
     corners
      of the night.
       Flicker, flash,
        near and far,
         turn on lamps,
          & sprinkle stars.
           One small flame,
            a tiny spark . . .
             or wide as day,
              you scatter dark.

18

SOFT-BOILED
Russell Hoban

I do not like the way you slide,
I do not like your soft inside,
I do not like you many ways,
And I could do for many days
Without a soft-boiled egg.

WARNING TO A FORK
Marjorie Maddox

Pitchfork for pie,
trident for tuna salad,
savior of sticky fingers,
heed my dishwasher's voice:
steer clear of the electric disposal,
mangler of metal utensils,
mortuary of soup spoons and knives.

I am young but a wise witness.
I've heard the clank and crunch,
the torture chamber for leftovers
churn and churn. Burn this
into your stainless steel mind:
the left sink is death,
a black hole with sharp teeth.
BEWARE! You will never
spear lettuce again!

BUFFALO
Penny Harter

Heavy as petrified wood
you stare from the rock face,
slow body aging in the moonlight,
feet lost in crevices.

You sniff the air.
It is not the same wind
you remember.
Your mouth is as cold
as the sky.

BISON
Kristine O'Connell George

You're not easy to love
  not someone I'd want to hug
  or take home with me.
Shaggy, with a very bad
  upholstery job,
  you're not a lighthearted animal.

Yet, when I look
  into your cloudy eyes
  you seem to be trying
to remember something,
  something important
  you need to tell me.

TO A SNOWFLAKE
X. J. Kennedy

You stand still in midair
As though you just can't quite
Make up your wisher where
You wish to spend tonight.

HAT HAIR
Joan Bransfield Graham

HEY, HAT . . .
you gave me
"hat hair,"
a sweat band,
a halo—bent,
it's evident
that once upon
my head there sat—*a hat.*

25

LETTER POEM TO A MAILBOX
Marjorie Maddox

Dear blue-suited sir,

How many luscious love letters
have you swallowed
and not a single line for you?

How many birthday cards digested?
Or bills crammed down
your metal throat?

You clank but never complain,
jaw stiff but not jealous.

What confidence you exude,
solid in concrete,
punctual pen pal of the post,
never a grudge when we take you for granted.

You are our fine, steel hero,
the destination of all walks,
friend of fickle weather
and marathon mailmen.

O Protector of our Epistles,
we salute you with stamps
and lipstick kisses, with effusive postscripts
and elaborate wax seals.

This one's for you.

In our humble wood homes,
we wait expectantly
for your scripted reply.

BEE, I'M EXPECTING YOU!
Emily Dickinson

Bee, I'm expecting you!
Was saying yesterday
To somebody you know
That you were due.

The frogs got home last week,
Are settled and at work,
Birds mostly back,
The clover warm and thick.

You'll get my letter by
The seventeenth; reply,
Or better, be with me.
Yours,
Fly.

STRAIGHT TALK
Nikki Grimes

Look, Bee
Fair is fair.
I don't burst into
Your honeycomb
Willy-nilly
Or interrupt you
While you feed on
Rose and Lily
So leave me alone, drone
Show yourself the door
And don't come
Buzzing round here
Anymore

DEAR SHELL
Karla Kuskin

Dear shell:
You curve extremely well.
And when I put you to my curving ear
and hear a whispered wind
far off
I cannot tell but it might be the sea.

Dear shell:
You also smell.

CONCH SHELL
Beverly McLoughland

In what wild garden
were you grown?

What wizard's spell
has turned
your wide pink-petalled blossom
into stone?

THE OCTOPUS
Ogden Nash

Tell me, O Octopus, I begs,
Is those things arms, or is they legs?
I marvel at thee, Octopus;
If I were thou, I'd call me Us.

THE SEA HORSE
Douglas Florian

You have
No hooves.
You have no hair.
You don't eat oats.
You don't breathe air.
You hatch from eggs.
You cannot race.
(You have no legs
With which to chase.)
You're not a colt
Nor mare
Nor filly.
You're called a horse.
I call that silly.

SKYSCRAPER
Dennis Lee

Skyscraper, skyscraper,
Scrape me some sky:
Tickle the sun
While the stars go by.

Tickle the stars
While the sun's climbing high,
Then skyscraper, skyscraper,
Scrape me some sky.

WHAT ARE YOU DOING?
Charles Reznikoff

What are you doing in our street among the automobiles, horse?
How are your cousins, the centaur and the unicorn?

WHISPERS TO THE WALL

Vietnam Veterans Memorial Washington, D.C. Dedicated 1982

Rebecca Kai Dotlich

You are him from Maine,
him, from Montana,
and every him from sea
to sea and back.
Stewart, Kelly, York;
you are all of those,
who shrimped on boats,
flew planes,
studied, wrote,
collected,
kissed.

The brave ones spill
across your face;
an indelible trace
of young sons
who played baseball,
cards, guitars.
Thompson, Sanchez, Vance;
you know their favorite dish,
their first romance.

On silent nights, do they tell you
of boyhoods and Beatles,
bruised knees and hearts,
birthdays missed . . .
those who shrimped on boats,
flew planes,
studied, wrote,
collected,
kissed.

HELLO, MOON!
Patricia Hubbell

Moon,
your reflection
is a tambourine,
shaking
in the lake's ripples

You are the nightsong of the sun—
Sometimes a full round note,
Sometimes a high thin *plink*
plucked on a hidden guitar

Moon,
you have seen the dinosaurs
sleeping
in their fern beds—
Do you see me,
stretched beneath
my flowered quilt?

Moon,
did I ever tell you
that sometimes
(I'm sorry, moon, but . . .)
you look like a . . .
    banana!

HELLO, BLACK HOLE
J. Patrick Lewis

Old black hOle,

Too fat to hang
Far out in space,
You'll pop—and BANG!

Your insides get
So blazing hot—
One day you're there,
The next you're not!

And no one knows
Exactly why
But in the ceiling
Of the sky,

Black hOle, you swallow

Starry light
As big as day
And black as night.